SECURITY

VISITOR LOG & SIGN IN BOOK

VISITORS

PLEASE CHECK-IN BEFORE SIGNING BELOW.

DATE	VISITOR'S NAME	REASON FOR VISIT	TIME IN	TIME OUT	SIGN / INITIAL

VISITORS

PLEASE CHECK-IN BEFORE SIGNING BELOW.

DATE	VISITOR'S NAME	REASON FOR VISIT	TIME IN	TIME OUT	SIGN / INITIAL

VISITORS

PLEASE CHECK-IN BEFORE SIGNING BELOW.

DATE	VISITOR'S NAME	REASON FOR VISIT	TIME IN	TIME OUT	SIGN / INITIAL

VISITORS

PLEASE CHECK-IN BEFORE SIGNING BELOW.

DATE	VISITOR'S NAME	REASON FOR VISIT	TIME IN	TIME OUT	SIGN / INITIAL

VISITORS

PLEASE CHECK-IN BEFORE SIGNING BELOW.

DATE	VISITOR'S NAME	REASON FOR VISIT	TIME IN	TIME OUT	SIGN / INITIAL

VISITORS

PLEASE CHECK-IN BEFORE SIGNING BELOW.

DATE	VISITOR'S NAME	REASON FOR VISIT	TIME IN	TIME OUT	SIGN / INITIAL

VISITORS

PLEASE CHECK-IN BEFORE SIGNING BELOW.

DATE	VISITOR'S NAME	REASON FOR VISIT	TIME IN	TIME OUT	SIGN / INITIAL

VISITORS

PLEASE CHECK-IN BEFORE SIGNING BELOW.

DATE	VISITOR'S NAME	REASON FOR VISIT	TIME IN	TIME OUT	SIGN / INITIAL

VISITORS

PLEASE CHECK-IN BEFORE SIGNING BELOW.

DATE	VISITOR'S NAME	REASON FOR VISIT	TIME IN	TIME OUT	SIGN / INITIAL

VISITORS

PLEASE CHECK-IN BEFORE SIGNING BELOW.

DATE	VISITOR'S NAME	REASON FOR VISIT	TIME IN	TIME OUT	SIGN / INITIAL

VISITORS

PLEASE CHECK-IN BEFORE SIGNING BELOW.

DATE	VISITOR'S NAME	REASON FOR VISIT	TIME IN	TIME OUT	SIGN / INITIAL

VISITORS

PLEASE CHECK-IN BEFORE SIGNING BELOW.

DATE	VISITOR'S NAME	REASON FOR VISIT	TIME IN	TIME OUT	SIGN / INITIAL

VISITORS

PLEASE CHECK-IN BEFORE SIGNING BELOW.

DATE	VISITOR'S NAME	REASON FOR VISIT	TIME IN	TIME OUT	SIGN / INITIAL

VISITORS

PLEASE CHECK-IN BEFORE SIGNING BELOW.

DATE	VISITOR'S NAME	REASON FOR VISIT	TIME IN	TIME OUT	SIGN / INITIAL

VISITORS

PLEASE CHECK-IN BEFORE SIGNING BELOW.

DATE	VISITOR'S NAME	REASON FOR VISIT	TIME IN	TIME OUT	SIGN / INITIAL

VISITORS

PLEASE CHECK-IN BEFORE SIGNING BELOW.

DATE	VISITOR'S NAME	REASON FOR VISIT	TIME IN	TIME OUT	SIGN / INITIAL

VISITORS

PLEASE CHECK-IN BEFORE SIGNING BELOW.

DATE	VISITOR'S NAME	REASON FOR VISIT	TIME IN	TIME OUT	SIGN / INITIAL

VISITORS

PLEASE CHECK-IN BEFORE SIGNING BELOW.

DATE	VISITOR'S NAME	REASON FOR VISIT	TIME IN	TIME OUT	SIGN / INITIAL

VISITORS

PLEASE CHECK-IN BEFORE SIGNING BELOW.

DATE	VISITOR'S NAME	REASON FOR VISIT	TIME IN	TIME OUT	SIGN / INITIAL

VISITORS

PLEASE CHECK-IN BEFORE SIGNING BELOW.

DATE	VISITOR'S NAME	REASON FOR VISIT	TIME IN	TIME OUT	SIGN / INITIAL

VISITORS

PLEASE CHECK-IN BEFORE SIGNING BELOW.

DATE	VISITOR'S NAME	REASON FOR VISIT	TIME IN	TIME OUT	SIGN / INITIAL

VISITORS

PLEASE CHECK-IN BEFORE SIGNING BELOW.

DATE	VISITOR'S NAME	REASON FOR VISIT	TIME IN	TIME OUT	SIGN / INITIAL

VISITORS

PLEASE CHECK-IN BEFORE SIGNING BELOW.

DATE	VISITOR'S NAME	REASON FOR VISIT	TIME IN	TIME OUT	SIGN / INITIAL

VISITORS

PLEASE CHECK-IN BEFORE SIGNING BELOW.

DATE	VISITOR'S NAME	REASON FOR VISIT	TIME IN	TIME OUT	SIGN / INITIAL

VISITORS

PLEASE CHECK-IN BEFORE SIGNING BELOW.

DATE	VISITOR'S NAME	REASON FOR VISIT	TIME IN	TIME OUT	SIGN / INITIAL

VISITORS

PLEASE CHECK-IN BEFORE SIGNING BELOW.

DATE	VISITOR'S NAME	REASON FOR VISIT	TIME IN	TIME OUT	SIGN / INITIAL

VISITORS

PLEASE CHECK-IN BEFORE SIGNING BELOW.

DATE	VISITOR'S NAME	REASON FOR VISIT	TIME IN	TIME OUT	SIGN / INITIAL

VISITORS

PLEASE CHECK-IN BEFORE SIGNING BELOW.

DATE	VISITOR'S NAME	REASON FOR VISIT	TIME IN	TIME OUT	SIGN / INITIAL

VISITORS

PLEASE CHECK-IN BEFORE SIGNING BELOW.

DATE	VISITOR'S NAME	REASON FOR VISIT	TIME IN	TIME OUT	SIGN / INITIAL

VISITORS

PLEASE CHECK-IN BEFORE SIGNING BELOW.

DATE	VISITOR'S NAME	REASON FOR VISIT	TIME IN	TIME OUT	SIGN / INITIAL

VISITORS

PLEASE CHECK-IN BEFORE SIGNING BELOW.

DATE	VISITOR'S NAME	REASON FOR VISIT	TIME IN	TIME OUT	SIGN / INITIAL

VISITORS

PLEASE CHECK-IN BEFORE SIGNING BELOW.

DATE	VISITOR'S NAME	REASON FOR VISIT	TIME IN	TIME OUT	SIGN / INITIAL

VISITORS

PLEASE CHECK-IN BEFORE SIGNING BELOW.

DATE	VISITOR'S NAME	REASON FOR VISIT	TIME IN	TIME OUT	SIGN / INITIAL

VISITORS

PLEASE CHECK-IN BEFORE SIGNING BELOW.

DATE	VISITOR'S NAME	REASON FOR VISIT	TIME IN	TIME OUT	SIGN / INITIAL

VISITORS

PLEASE CHECK-IN BEFORE SIGNING BELOW.

DATE	VISITOR'S NAME	REASON FOR VISIT	TIME IN	TIME OUT	SIGN / INITIAL

VISITORS

PLEASE CHECK-IN BEFORE SIGNING BELOW.

DATE	VISITOR'S NAME	REASON FOR VISIT	TIME IN	TIME OUT	SIGN / INITIAL

VISITORS

PLEASE CHECK-IN BEFORE SIGNING BELOW.

DATE	VISITOR'S NAME	REASON FOR VISIT	TIME IN	TIME OUT	SIGN / INITIAL

VISITORS

PLEASE CHECK-IN BEFORE SIGNING BELOW.

DATE	VISITOR'S NAME	REASON FOR VISIT	TIME IN	TIME OUT	SIGN / INITIAL

VISITORS

PLEASE CHECK-IN BEFORE SIGNING BELOW.

DATE	VISITOR'S NAME	REASON FOR VISIT	TIME IN	TIME OUT	SIGN / INITIAL

VISITORS

PLEASE CHECK-IN BEFORE SIGNING BELOW.

DATE	VISITOR'S NAME	REASON FOR VISIT	TIME IN	TIME OUT	SIGN / INITIAL

VISITORS

PLEASE CHECK-IN BEFORE SIGNING BELOW.

DATE	VISITOR'S NAME	REASON FOR VISIT	TIME IN	TIME OUT	SIGN / INITIAL

VISITORS

PLEASE CHECK-IN BEFORE SIGNING BELOW.

DATE	VISITOR'S NAME	REASON FOR VISIT	TIME IN	TIME OUT	SIGN / INITIAL

VISITORS

PLEASE CHECK-IN BEFORE SIGNING BELOW.

DATE	VISITOR'S NAME	REASON FOR VISIT	TIME IN	TIME OUT	SIGN / INITIAL

VISITORS

PLEASE CHECK-IN BEFORE SIGNING BELOW.

DATE	VISITOR'S NAME	REASON FOR VISIT	TIME IN	TIME OUT	SIGN / INITIAL

VISITORS

PLEASE CHECK-IN BEFORE SIGNING BELOW.

DATE	VISITOR'S NAME	REASON FOR VISIT	TIME IN	TIME OUT	SIGN / INITIAL

VISITORS

PLEASE CHECK-IN BEFORE SIGNING BELOW.

DATE	VISITOR'S NAME	REASON FOR VISIT	TIME IN	TIME OUT	SIGN / INITIAL

VISITORS

PLEASE CHECK-IN BEFORE SIGNING BELOW.

DATE	VISITOR'S NAME	REASON FOR VISIT	TIME IN	TIME OUT	SIGN / INITIAL

VISITORS

PLEASE CHECK-IN BEFORE SIGNING BELOW.

DATE	VISITOR'S NAME	REASON FOR VISIT	TIME IN	TIME OUT	SIGN / INITIAL

VISITORS

PLEASE CHECK-IN BEFORE SIGNING BELOW.

DATE	VISITOR'S NAME	REASON FOR VISIT	TIME IN	TIME OUT	SIGN / INITIAL

VISITORS

PLEASE CHECK-IN BEFORE SIGNING BELOW.

DATE	VISITOR'S NAME	REASON FOR VISIT	TIME IN	TIME OUT	SIGN / INITIAL

VISITORS

PLEASE CHECK-IN BEFORE SIGNING BELOW.

DATE	VISITOR'S NAME	REASON FOR VISIT	TIME IN	TIME OUT	SIGN / INITIAL

VISITORS

PLEASE CHECK-IN BEFORE SIGNING BELOW.

DATE	VISITOR'S NAME	REASON FOR VISIT	TIME IN	TIME OUT	SIGN / INITIAL

VISITORS

PLEASE CHECK-IN BEFORE SIGNING BELOW.

DATE	VISITOR'S NAME	REASON FOR VISIT	TIME IN	TIME OUT	SIGN / INITIAL

VISITORS

PLEASE CHECK-IN BEFORE SIGNING BELOW.

DATE	VISITOR'S NAME	REASON FOR VISIT	TIME IN	TIME OUT	SIGN / INITIAL
DATE	VISITOR'S NAME	REASON FOR VISIT	TIME IN	TIME OUT	SIGN / INITIAL

VISITORS

PLEASE CHECK-IN BEFORE SIGNING BELOW.

DATE	VISITOR'S NAME	REASON FOR VISIT	TIME IN	TIME OUT	SIGN / INITIAL

VISITORS

PLEASE CHECK-IN BEFORE SIGNING BELOW.

DATE	VISITOR'S NAME	REASON FOR VISIT	TIME IN	TIME OUT	SIGN / INITIAL

VISITORS

PLEASE CHECK-IN BEFORE SIGNING BELOW.

DATE	VISITOR'S NAME	REASON FOR VISIT	TIME IN	TIME OUT	SIGN / INITIAL

VISITORS

PLEASE CHECK-IN BEFORE SIGNING BELOW.

DATE	VISITOR'S NAME	REASON FOR VISIT	TIME IN	TIME OUT	SIGN / INITIAL

VISITORS

PLEASE CHECK-IN BEFORE SIGNING BELOW.

DATE	VISITOR'S NAME	REASON FOR VISIT	TIME IN	TIME OUT	SIGN / INITIAL

VISITORS

PLEASE CHECK-IN BEFORE SIGNING BELOW.

DATE	VISITOR'S NAME	REASON FOR VISIT	TIME IN	TIME OUT	SIGN / INITIAL

VISITORS

PLEASE CHECK-IN BEFORE SIGNING BELOW.

DATE	VISITOR'S NAME	REASON FOR VISIT	TIME IN	TIME OUT	SIGN / INITIAL

VISITORS

PLEASE CHECK-IN BEFORE SIGNING BELOW.

DATE	VISITOR'S NAME	REASON FOR VISIT	TIME IN	TIME OUT	SIGN / INITIAL

VISITORS

PLEASE CHECK-IN BEFORE SIGNING BELOW.

DATE	VISITOR'S NAME	REASON FOR VISIT	TIME IN	TIME OUT	SIGN / INITIAL

VISITORS

PLEASE CHECK-IN BEFORE SIGNING BELOW.

DATE	VISITOR'S NAME	REASON FOR VISIT	TIME IN	TIME OUT	SIGN / INITIAL

VISITORS

PLEASE CHECK-IN BEFORE SIGNING BELOW.

DATE	VISITOR'S NAME	REASON FOR VISIT	TIME IN	TIME OUT	SIGN / INITIAL

VISITORS

PLEASE CHECK-IN BEFORE SIGNING BELOW.

DATE	VISITOR'S NAME	REASON FOR VISIT	TIME IN	TIME OUT	SIGN / INITIAL

VISITORS

PLEASE CHECK-IN BEFORE SIGNING BELOW.

DATE	VISITOR'S NAME	REASON FOR VISIT	TIME IN	TIME OUT	SIGN / INITIAL

VISITORS

PLEASE CHECK-IN BEFORE SIGNING BELOW.

DATE	VISITOR'S NAME	REASON FOR VISIT	TIME IN	TIME OUT	SIGN / INITIAL

VISITORS

PLEASE CHECK-IN BEFORE SIGNING BELOW.

DATE	VISITOR'S NAME	REASON FOR VISIT	TIME IN	TIME OUT	SIGN / INITIAL

VISITORS

PLEASE CHECK-IN BEFORE SIGNING BELOW.

DATE	VISITOR'S NAME	REASON FOR VISIT	TIME IN	TIME OUT	SIGN / INITIAL

VISITORS

PLEASE CHECK-IN BEFORE SIGNING BELOW.

DATE	VISITOR'S NAME	REASON FOR VISIT	TIME IN	TIME OUT	SIGN / INITIAL

VISITORS

PLEASE CHECK-IN BEFORE SIGNING BELOW.

DATE	VISITOR'S NAME	REASON FOR VISIT	TIME IN	TIME OUT	SIGN / INITIAL

VISITORS

PLEASE CHECK-IN BEFORE SIGNING BELOW.

DATE	VISITOR'S NAME	REASON FOR VISIT	TIME IN	TIME OUT	SIGN / INITIAL

VISITORS

PLEASE CHECK-IN BEFORE SIGNING BELOW.

DATE	VISITOR'S NAME	REASON FOR VISIT	TIME IN	TIME OUT	SIGN / INITIAL

VISITORS

PLEASE CHECK-IN BEFORE SIGNING BELOW.

DATE	VISITOR'S NAME	REASON FOR VISIT	TIME IN	TIME OUT	SIGN / INITIAL

VISITORS

PLEASE CHECK-IN BEFORE SIGNING BELOW.

DATE	VISITOR'S NAME	REASON FOR VISIT	TIME IN	TIME OUT	SIGN / INITIAL

VISITORS

PLEASE CHECK-IN BEFORE SIGNING BELOW.

DATE	VISITOR'S NAME	REASON FOR VISIT	TIME IN	TIME OUT	SIGN / INITIAL

VISITORS

PLEASE CHECK-IN BEFORE SIGNING BELOW.

DATE	VISITOR'S NAME	REASON FOR VISIT	TIME IN	TIME OUT	SIGN / INITIAL

VISITORS

PLEASE CHECK-IN BEFORE SIGNING BELOW.

DATE	VISITOR'S NAME	REASON FOR VISIT	TIME IN	TIME OUT	SIGN / INITIAL

VISITORS

PLEASE CHECK-IN BEFORE SIGNING BELOW.

DATE	VISITOR'S NAME	REASON FOR VISIT	TIME IN	TIME OUT	SIGN / INITIAL

VISITORS

PLEASE CHECK-IN BEFORE SIGNING BELOW.

DATE	VISITOR'S NAME	REASON FOR VISIT	TIME IN	TIME OUT	SIGN / INITIAL

VISITORS

PLEASE CHECK-IN BEFORE SIGNING BELOW.

DATE	VISITOR'S NAME	REASON FOR VISIT	TIME IN	TIME OUT	SIGN / INITIAL

VISITORS

PLEASE CHECK-IN BEFORE SIGNING BELOW.

DATE	VISITOR'S NAME	REASON FOR VISIT	TIME IN	TIME OUT	SIGN / INITIAL

VISITORS

PLEASE CHECK-IN BEFORE SIGNING BELOW.

DATE	VISITOR'S NAME	REASON FOR VISIT	TIME IN	TIME OUT	SIGN / INITIAL

VISITORS

PLEASE CHECK-IN BEFORE SIGNING BELOW.

DATE	VISITOR'S NAME	REASON FOR VISIT	TIME IN	TIME OUT	SIGN / INITIAL

VISITORS

PLEASE CHECK-IN BEFORE SIGNING BELOW.

DATE	VISITOR'S NAME	REASON FOR VISIT	TIME IN	TIME OUT	SIGN / INITIAL

VISITORS

PLEASE CHECK-IN BEFORE SIGNING BELOW.

DATE	VISITOR'S NAME	REASON FOR VISIT	TIME IN	TIME OUT	SIGN / INITIAL

VISITORS

PLEASE CHECK-IN BEFORE SIGNING BELOW.

DATE	VISITOR'S NAME	REASON FOR VISIT	TIME IN	TIME OUT	SIGN / INITIAL

VISITORS

PLEASE CHECK-IN BEFORE SIGNING BELOW.

DATE	VISITOR'S NAME	REASON FOR VISIT	TIME IN	TIME OUT	SIGN / INITIAL

VISITORS

PLEASE CHECK-IN BEFORE SIGNING BELOW.

DATE	VISITOR'S NAME	REASON FOR VISIT	TIME IN	TIME OUT	SIGN / INITIAL

VISITORS

PLEASE CHECK-IN BEFORE SIGNING BELOW.

DATE	VISITOR'S NAME	REASON FOR VISIT	TIME IN	TIME OUT	SIGN / INITIAL

VISITORS

PLEASE CHECK-IN BEFORE SIGNING BELOW.

DATE	VISITOR'S NAME	REASON FOR VISIT	TIME IN	TIME OUT	SIGN / INITIAL

VISITORS

PLEASE CHECK-IN BEFORE SIGNING BELOW.

DATE	VISITOR'S NAME	REASON FOR VISIT	TIME IN	TIME OUT	SIGN / INITIAL

VISITORS

PLEASE CHECK-IN BEFORE SIGNING BELOW.

DATE	VISITOR'S NAME	REASON FOR VISIT	TIME IN	TIME OUT	SIGN / INITIAL

VISITORS

PLEASE CHECK-IN BEFORE SIGNING BELOW.

DATE	VISITOR'S NAME	REASON FOR VISIT	TIME IN	TIME OUT	SIGN / INITIAL

VISITORS

PLEASE CHECK-IN BEFORE SIGNING BELOW.

DATE	VISITOR'S NAME	REASON FOR VISIT	TIME IN	TIME OUT	SIGN / INITIAL

VISITORS

PLEASE CHECK-IN BEFORE SIGNING BELOW.

DATE	VISITOR'S NAME	REASON FOR VISIT	TIME IN	TIME OUT	SIGN / INITIAL

VISITORS

PLEASE CHECK-IN BEFORE SIGNING BELOW.

DATE	VISITOR'S NAME	REASON FOR VISIT	TIME IN	TIME OUT	SIGN / INITIAL

VISITORS

PLEASE CHECK-IN BEFORE SIGNING BELOW.

DATE	VISITOR'S NAME	REASON FOR VISIT	TIME IN	TIME OUT	SIGN / INITIAL

VISITORS

PLEASE CHECK-IN BEFORE SIGNING BELOW.

DATE	VISITOR'S NAME	REASON FOR VISIT	TIME IN	TIME OUT	SIGN / INITIAL

VISITORS

PLEASE CHECK-IN BEFORE SIGNING BELOW.

DATE	VISITOR'S NAME	REASON FOR VISIT	TIME IN	TIME OUT	SIGN / INITIAL

VISITORS

PLEASE CHECK-IN BEFORE SIGNING BELOW.

DATE	VISITOR'S NAME	REASON FOR VISIT	TIME IN	TIME OUT	SIGN / INITIAL

VISITORS

PLEASE CHECK-IN BEFORE SIGNING BELOW.

DATE	VISITOR'S NAME	REASON FOR VISIT	TIME IN	TIME OUT	SIGN / INITIAL

VISITORS

PLEASE CHECK-IN BEFORE SIGNING BELOW.

DATE	VISITOR'S NAME	REASON FOR VISIT	TIME IN	TIME OUT	SIGN / INITIAL

VISITORS

PLEASE CHECK-IN BEFORE SIGNING BELOW.

DATE	VISITOR'S NAME	REASON FOR VISIT	TIME IN	TIME OUT	SIGN / INITIAL

VISITORS

PLEASE CHECK-IN BEFORE SIGNING BELOW.

DATE	VISITOR'S NAME	REASON FOR VISIT	TIME IN	TIME OUT	SIGN / INITIAL

VISITORS

PLEASE CHECK-IN BEFORE SIGNING BELOW.

DATE	VISITOR'S NAME	REASON FOR VISIT	TIME IN	TIME OUT	SIGN / INITIAL

VISITORS

PLEASE CHECK-IN BEFORE SIGNING BELOW.

DATE	VISITOR'S NAME	REASON FOR VISIT	TIME IN	TIME OUT	SIGN / INITIAL

VISITORS

PLEASE CHECK-IN BEFORE SIGNING BELOW.

DATE	VISITOR'S NAME	REASON FOR VISIT	TIME IN	TIME OUT	SIGN / INITIAL

VISITORS

PLEASE CHECK-IN BEFORE SIGNING BELOW.

DATE	VISITOR'S NAME	REASON FOR VISIT	TIME IN	TIME OUT	SIGN / INITIAL

VISITORS

PLEASE CHECK-IN BEFORE SIGNING BELOW.

DATE	VISITOR'S NAME	REASON FOR VISIT	TIME IN	TIME OUT	SIGN / INITIAL

VISITORS

PLEASE CHECK-IN BEFORE SIGNING BELOW.

DATE	VISITOR'S NAME	REASON FOR VISIT	TIME IN	TIME OUT	SIGN / INITIAL

VISITORS

PLEASE CHECK-IN BEFORE SIGNING BELOW.

DATE	VISITOR'S NAME	REASON FOR VISIT	TIME IN	TIME OUT	SIGN / INITIAL

VISITORS

PLEASE CHECK-IN BEFORE SIGNING BELOW.

DATE	VISITOR'S NAME	REASON FOR VISIT	TIME IN	TIME OUT	SIGN / INITIAL

VISITORS

PLEASE CHECK-IN BEFORE SIGNING BELOW.

DATE	VISITOR'S NAME	REASON FOR VISIT	TIME IN	TIME OUT	SIGN / INITIAL

VISITORS

PLEASE CHECK-IN BEFORE SIGNING BELOW.

DATE	VISITOR'S NAME	REASON FOR VISIT	TIME IN	TIME OUT	SIGN / INITIAL

VISITORS

PLEASE CHECK-IN BEFORE SIGNING BELOW.

DATE	VISITOR'S NAME	REASON FOR VISIT	TIME IN	TIME OUT	SIGN / INITIAL

Made in the USA
Middletown, DE
04 March 2025